Original title:
Blooming Beginnings

Copyright © 2025 Creative Arts Management OÜ
All rights reserved.

Author: Riley Donovan
ISBN HARDBACK: 978-1-80566-793-3
ISBN PAPERBACK: 978-1-80566-813-8

The Whisper of New Leaves

Tiny buds peek out with glee,
Waving like they're texting me.
They giggle in the morning dew,
"We're here! How about you?"

Branches crack, a comical scene,
Got a chirpy squad, oh so keen!
Squirrels twirl in a dizzy dance,
Giving springtime a whacky chance.

First Light in the Meadow

Sunlight tickles the grassy tips,
While daisies show off their sunny flips.
A rabbit sneezes, jumps in a fright,
"Oops! Didn't see you, not my night!"

Butterflies dress in polka dots,
Wobbling like they forgot their spots.
The daisies giggle, the clovers cheer,
As the morning sings without a fear.

Unfurling Dreams

Little petals stretch and yawn,
Saying, "Finally, the dark is gone!"
They tickle each other, what a show,
Winking at bees down below.

A sleepy bud lets out a grin,
"Watch me now, gonna bust right in!"
The garden laughs, all full of charms,
As new life flashes silly arms.

A Canvas of Fresh Colors

Splash of yellow, dab of green,
Every hue a playful scene.
Crayons giggle in the sun's warm ray,
"Let's color the world, hip-hip-hooray!"

A purple flower sings a tune,
"Wonder how the sun feels by noon?"
While tulips sway in a funky beat,
Dancing shoes on their tiny feet.

Seeds of Tomorrow

Tiny seeds in the dirt,
Wiggling like they're nervous,
Waiting for the sun's warm hug,
Poking heads out, feeling rich.

Worms are dancing, what a sight,
Squirrels plot their nutty flight,
Flowers giggle when they sprout,
Heaven help us, there's no doubt!

Embracing the New Light

Morning rays make shadows play,
Coffee cups cheer up the day,
My plants shout, 'We're wide awake!'
Watch out world, here comes the cake!

Butterflies wear polka dots,
The bees buzz with little plots,
Laughter tickles petals' seams,
All aboard the sunshine dreams!

Reflections in Springtime

Puddles splash with silly glee,
Jumping frogs sing harmony,
Mirrors of the sky above,
Reflecting all that silly love.

Daffodils with faces bright,
Challenge clouds to a pillow fight,
Chirping birds, a cheeky crew,
Remind us all to sing anew!

The Unfolding Canvas

A canvas stretched for all to see,
Colors dancing wild and free,
Brushes tickle blooms in rows,
Even skies have funny prose.

Nature splashes with delight,
Every day feels just so right,
The world's a gallery of cheer,
Imagine that—a pop-up sphere!

Awakening the Earth

The worms are wiggling with cheer,
As flowers start to disappear,
They're hiding under the soil's hug,
While ducks engage in a silly tug.

The sprouts are popping with delight,
Dancing petals, quite a sight,
While grass tickles toes that roam,
It's a funny little call to home.

The Soft Rise of Green

The trees are yawning, stretching high,
With squirrels chasing clouds in the sky,
A ladybug dons a tiny vest,
Feeling fancy; oh, what a quest!

The daffodils wear wacky hats,
While frogs hop like acrobats,
The sun peeks out to say hello,
And all the critters start the show!

First Notes of Spring

The robins sing a cheeky tune,
While bunnies bounce beneath the moon,
A daisy winks at passing bees,
It's quite the fragrant, funny tease!

The wind carries whispers of jest,
Encouraging flowers to dress their best,
While children giggle at nature's game,
Spring's antics are never the same.

When the World Renewed

The raindrops play a splishy song,
Puddles jump; they can't be wrong,
The sun appears with a silly grin,
As frogs in chorus joyfully spin.

New shoots peek out, like little spies,
With bugs that wear oversized ties,
The world's a stage, it's quite bizarre,
In nature's circus, we're all the stars!

Petals in the Wind

In the garden where chaos reigns,
Tulips argue over window panes.
Daisies giggle at the bees' dance,
While roses plot their floral romance.

A snickering crow steals a worm,
While sunflowers stretch, trying to squirm.
A ladybug slips on a dew drop,
As nature prepares for the fun nonstop.

The butterflies wear mismatched socks,
And ants march in line for their blocks.
With petals drifting like silly hats,
Even weeds join the party, imagine that!

When colors explode and laughter sings,
Every blossom knows the joy it brings.
So here's to the garden, wacky and bright,
Where silliness reigns from morning till night.

Spring's Gentle Ballet

The flowers twirl in a breezy show,
As raindrops giggle and rivers flow.
Squirrels practice their acrobats,
While frogs wear tuxedos and dance on mats.

A plucky bud leaps with flair and grace,
But stumbles hard, falls flat on its face!
Nearby, a snail joins in the fun,
Saying 'I'll win the race, just wait, I'm not done!'

The sunshine claps at this quirky play,
As clouds sport mustaches and drift away.
Each petal ticks like a funny clock,
While the grass giggles, tickled by a rock.

So let's waltz through the vibrant scene,
With nature's jokes and a laugh in between.
For in this ballet of life so spry,
Even the worms wear funky ties.

Whispers of Renewal

The crocus pops up with a sly grin,
Whispering secrets where the grass has been.
A busy bee buzzes with a quirky hum,
While daisies are just waiting to come.

The tulips chatter in colors so bright,
Plotting their outfits for the spring night.
With petals like skirts, they twist and sway,
While bunnies hop in a comedic display.

A frog croaks sonnets with a grand croak,
As butterflies giggle at the silly folk.
Nature's giggles fall like soft rain,
As every creature dances in gain.

The trees give a shake and shake off the dust,
As the world awakens, in laughter we trust.
So here's to the whispers, all funny and light,
In a springtime frolic, a joyous delight.

The Awakening Dawn

As the dawn peeks in with a sleepy yawn,
Morning glories greet it with a scrawn.
A rooster crows with a wobbly cheer,
While daffodils wink as they draw near.

The sun tickles tulips with a warm light,
As squirrels work on their morning height.
A lazy bumblebee takes a stretch,
With nectar dreams only they can fetch.

The daisies gossip, sharing a laugh,
While the wind gives them a rascally half.
With puddles dancing under little feet,
They stomp around for a giggly beat.

So let's toast to the new day's air,
Where laughter grows in the morning glare.
Nature's jesters line up in a row,
For in each sunrise, endless fun will grow.

The First Glimmer of Tomorrow

A sprout peeked out with a little grin,
Said, 'Look at me, I'm ready to begin!'
With sunshine hats and raindrop shoes,
It danced in circles, shaking off the snooze.

A worm rolled by, gave a playful shout,
'You won't believe what it's all about!'
The breeze chimed in with a tickling laugh,
Together they plotted a silly craft.

Rise of the Tender Shoots

Tiny leaves stretch with a goofy face,
They wear their colors, a wild embrace.
One said, 'I'm a tree!' with a mighty pose,
The other just snorted, 'Try again, you rose!'

As the sun peeks through, they start to sway,
One leaf shouted, 'Today's my play!'
They gathered round with a feathery cheer,
Complaining about sunlight too hot to bear!

Shadows of Dawn

The grass stretched out in a sleepy dance,
While the flowers whispered, 'Give us a chance!'
A daisy popped up, cracking a joke,
'I'm just a weed with high hopes, folks!'

Shadows painted tales of the night before,
With laughter that echoed from every pore.
A lizard in shades said, 'Get in the light!'
While dozing off, it snored, such a sight!

When the Earth Smiles

The soil chuckled, rich and warm,
'Let's grow something silly, let's break the norm!'
A tadpole jumped, heard the call,
'Join my party, we'll have a ball!'

So here's to the seedlings, all fresh and fun,
Throwing wild parties 'til day is done.
They twirled and they spun with no reason to pout,
In a garden of giggles, that's what it's about!

First Blossoms of a New Era

In a garden where cows like to chew,
Flowers giggle as they wave at the dew.
A squirrel in shades, so cool and suave,
Complains that his nuts are too far to stow.

First Blossoms of a New Era

The sun says hello with a wink and a grin,
While socks on the line have a dance-off to win.
Butterflies strut in their colorful clothes,
While bees rock the party, nobody knows.

First Blossoms of a New Era

A daffodil tripled up on caffeine,
Tells tulips a joke — it's a silly routine.
The daisies just giggle and roll on the ground,
While the whole garden's laughing; what joy can be found!

First Blossoms of a New Era

The sunflowers cheer, reaching up for the sky,
While the sprouts have a meeting to savor pie.
Critters all gather with a gleam in their eyes,
Opining that spring is a perfect surprise.

Whispers of the Earth's Heart

The mud puddles spark with a splash and a glee,
As children jump in, too eager to flee.
What joy in the squish, the gooey delight,
While worms laugh below, saying, 'What a sight!'

Whispers of the Earth's Heart

Trees tell tales to the wind with a shake,
Of acorns they've dropped, oh, what a mistake!
The grass dances lightly; it's tickling toes,
While daisies give dares to the shy little rose.

A New Chapter in Bloom

The daisies played poker, and who won the hand?
A clumsy old cactus took all the planned.
His prickles confused, they laughed till they cried,
While the wise old oak just watched, dignified.

A New Chapter in Bloom

The raindrops race down from leaves to the ground,
While frogs leap and croak, making quite the sound.
A puddle appears, and they all dive as one,
With splashes and laughs, oh what silly fun!

The Color of Renewal

The crayons all gathered in a box for a while,
And decided their colors should blend with a smile.
They splattered on canvases, wild and spree,
Said, 'Who needs a plan? Just be bold and free!'

The Color of Renewal

The rainbow talked trash with the clouds up high,
Said, 'I'm the trendsetter, the limit's the sky!'
While the sun painted gold on the world below,
The tulips just laughed in a colorful show.

The Symphony of Fresh Start

A trumpet blares, the tulips cheer,
A squirrel dances, let's make it clear!
The sun emerges, with a silly grin,
And all the flowers shout, "Let the fun begin!"

The daisies jig, the roses sway,
While birds form bands, in a bright array.
The earth provides a stage so wide,
For the goofiest blooms to come and bide.

In every garden, a joke's unspun,
As petals giggle in the warm, bold sun.
The shape of laughter fills the air,
With nature's tune, beyond compare!

So let's all join this flowery spree,
And dance along with glee, just you and me.
For every sprout has its own little part,
In the symphony of a brand-new start!

Nature's Confetti

Sprinkles of petals, tossed with delight,
Dandelions float, like kites in flight.
A cheerful breeze brings a giggling crowd,
As grasses sway, feeling rather proud.

The trees wear hats of fresh, green leaves,
While bees buzz around, "Oh, spring appeaves!"
With pops of color, they start to twirl,
As if to say, "Let's give it a whirl!"

Pollen parties throw themselves about,
While ants march in like a rebellious scout.
Twisty vines gain height with pure finesse,
Wearing vine hats in floral dress!

So paint the world in shades of bright,
With nature's chuckle, every day feels right.
For life's a festival of joy undenied,
With nature's confetti, let's laugh and glide!

Promises of the Spring Breeze

Whispers of winter start to fade away,
The breeze chuckles, coaxing blooms to play.
"Hey there, sunshine, it's time to shine!"
The flowers grin, knowing they'll be fine.

A daffodil winks, inviting a laugh,
While bumblebees do their silly staff.
With each gust, a tickle is felt,
As tulips dance, oh how they melt!

The clouds play peek-a-boo with the sky,
As if they're not just passing by.
Every breeze carries a funny tune,
Humorous whispers that say, "Soon, oh soon!"

So let's embrace this breezy jest,
Where every sprout knows to do its best.
For with a flutter, the world's alive,
In the promises that make laughter thrive!

The Dance of New Growth

Tiny seeds jump up with cheerful flair,
Saying, "We're sprouting, come dance if you dare!"
With a twist and a turn, the garden's alive,
In this wacky waltz, let's all dive!

Each little sprout wears a floppy hat,
Wiggling their roots, how silly is that?
Frogs join in, croaking songs to delight,
As petals giggle, oh what a sight!

The carrots do a cha-cha in line,
While peppers spin round, feeling just fine.
Even the weeds want to join the fun,
Saying, "We're here too, let's go, everyone!"

So grab your boots, let's dance in a row,
With every new shoot, there's so much to show.
For nature's a party, let it not cease,
In the dance of new growth, we find our peace!

Revelations in the Garden

In the dirt I found a shoe,
It tells tales of a worm or two.
The daisies giggle with delight,
As bees throw parties every night.

A potato dreams of being fries,
While radishes hide in little lies.
The carrots wear their leafy crowns,
As we have fun, let's flip the frowns.

Sunflowers sway, they've got the moves,
While the grasshopper busts some grooves.
Oh, the daisies whisper sweetly now,
What secrets hide? We'll find out how!

A garden gnome starts cracking jokes,
As he watches all the funny folks.
With hula hoops, we swing around,
In laughter's arms, we are surely found.

Hues of Hope

In the paintbox, colors play,
Turning drab to bright and gay.
A purple daffodil took flight,
And landed in a dandelion fight.

With one cheeky sprout wearing shades,
He claims, 'I'm the king of garden parades!'
The tulips laugh and show their bling,
"Join us now, it's a colorful fling!"

A rainbow made of herbs and thyme,
Dancing in rhythm, keeping time.
"Where's the party?" calls basil spry,
As mint replies with a curly fry!

The soil's bursting with tales untold,
Embracing weeds, both brave and bold.
A patchwork quilt of green and cheer,
In every sprout, we see the year.

Songs of the First Fragrance

Morning dew sings sweet and clear,
A ladybug struts, full of cheer.
"Who smells like cake?" asks the bee,
"Is frosting in that petal, for me?"

The lilacs hum a sprightly tune,
While violets plan a picnic soon.
"Let's dance and glide!" cries out the breeze,
As the pansies try to find their keys.

A worm writes lyrics, kind of weird,
About the sun that glows and cheered.
"Let's sprinkle laughter all around,
With every hop, make joy profound!"

The lilies roll their precious eyes,
At all the flirtations and the sighs.
Yet amidst the joy and fragrant air,
A rose winks, "Life's a vibrant affair!"

The Twinge of Awakening

The crocus popped up with a grin,
"Spring's the time to make a spin!"
With puzzled sprouts, they scratch their heads,
"Did you hear? It's time to spread!"

The grass stretches in contorted dreams,
Planning heists of pollen creams.
"Watch out for squirrels with tricky schemes,"
They laugh and plot in sunshine beams.

A butterfly sips on nectar sweet,
While ants march in unison, neat.
But oh! A sneeze disrupts the vibe,
And tulips giggle, "That's quite a tribe!"

As leaves unfold, the snickers rise,
The garden's filled with silly cries.
Embraced by laughter's sunny glow,
Awakening life—what a lovely show!

Echoes of the First Rain

A drop of water, plop, plop, plop,
Wakes up the seedlings, don't dare stop!
They wiggle and giggle, oh what a sight,
Dancing in puddles, pure delight!

The worms play charades, in the wet ground,
While ants throw a party, all around.
With tiny umbrellas, they march in line,
Celebrating the storm, it's party time!

Raindrops tap-dance on leaves so green,
The flowers chime in, it's quite the scene.
Bumblebees buzzing, join the parade,
A jolly procession, plans being made!

Then clouds play peek-a-boo, can't hide too long,
Sunbeams return, like a cheerful song.
With laughter and joy, nature's first cheer,
This is how fun really gets here!

Nature's Gentle Resurrection

Out of the ground, a sprout appears,
Tickled by sunshine and friendly cheers.
It shakes off the dirt, gives a big stretch,
Like a sleeping cat, it's found its fetch!

Daffodils don hats, they bloom with flair,
Whispering secrets to the cool spring air.
The bees are in on it, buzzing around,
Pretending to be lost, but they've found their ground!

Grass blades tickle the toes of the sun,
Singing a chorus, "Oh, this is fun!"
And ladybugs dance like they own the scene,
With polka dots shining, they reign as queens!

The breeze tells jokes to the flowers bright,
And soon every petal is laughing with light.
Nature's revival feels like a tease,
Just a little guffaw from the biggest trees!

Seeds of Tomorrow's Song

Tiny seeds whisper, "Let's make a plan,"
"I'll be a flower, you be a fan!"
They giggle and jostle, in cozy rows,
Excited for sunshine and warming glows!

"Hey, don't forget me, I'll sprout like a champ!"
Said a little acorn, "I'm a tree, not a lamp!"
With roots underground, they're all dreaming wide,
Imagining branches where squirrels can slide!

Mischievous dandelions, blown by the breeze,
Shouting, "Catch us, we're flying with ease!"
Giggles of grasshoppers hopping about,
Who knew the garden could be such a rout!

The sun rises up, it's a brand new day,
Every little sprout has its part to play.
Nature's sonnet, fun notes in the air,
Seeds finding rhythm, with flair and care!

Fresh Tapestry of Life

A canvas of colors, nature's delight,
Ribbons of petals, so wondrously bright.
Giggles of daisies, tipsy and free,
Spreading their joy, for all to see!

Each butterfly winks, flaunting its style,
With a flit and a flutter, it goes for a mile.
"Catch me if you can!" it teases the bees,
While the frogs croak tunes in the warm evening breeze.

Up high, in the trees, the squirrels hold court,
Throwing acorn parties, their favorite sport.
With pinecone hats and a dance so spry,
They laugh and they tumble, oh my, oh my!

Night arrives softly, with a wink and a sigh,
Stars start to twinkle in the big, velvet sky.
And as creatures snuggle, and day takes its stride,
Tomorrow awaits with a merry new ride!

The Quiet Surge of Life

In the garden, seeds said hi,
They twirled and danced, oh my!
A beetle stumbles, what a sight,
Wearing a hat—what a delight!

The daisies giggle, quite absurd,
They whisper secrets, not a word.
A snail on stilts, struts with flair,
While crickets cheer him from a chair.

Sunflowers stretch, touch the sky,
As butterflies tease, flying by.
A shy little sprout hums a tune,
Under the gaze of a smiling moon.

With each bud that cracks the ground,
Life's a party, look around!
Pots and petals, colors swirl,
Nature's antics in a whirl!

Tales from the Burgeoning

Once a seed thought he was cool,
Befriended a worm who played the fool.
They crafted capes from leaves they found,
And plotted mischief all around.

The tulips told tales of the rain,
While ants in suits danced on the lane.
A ladybug carried a briefcase, too,
Saying, 'Business first, fun's for a review!'

The roses laughed, wearing thorns,
Pretended to be rock stars, adorned.
A wise old oak observed the jest,
Said, 'In laughter, we are blessed.'

So the garden grows, week by week,
With curious friends, as they peek.
Each day's a story, some slightly wild,
Nature's funhouse, forever a child!

The Serene Awakening

In the morning, petals yawn,
Stretching wide, the light has dawned.
A hummingbird spills coffee beans,
While chatting with the bumblebees.

The ferns wear glasses, reading news,
While raccoons gossip in their shoes.
A dandelion painting snaps,
With critters posing, funny hats!

The sunflowers twirl in golden garb,
A big parade—it's not too far.
With laughter carried on the breeze,
The garden sings with jokes like these.

So if you wander where life's spry,
You'll find the cheer, just look up high.
For in the quiet, joy will seep,
In nature's laughter, secrets keep!

New Horizons Unfurled

A sprout breaks ground with a little pop,
It giggles loud, 'I'm on the top!'
Next to it, a weed's in shock,
Said, 'I'll never climb that rock!'

The clouds puff up, as if to boast,
'What's cooking down there? It's a roast!'
The worms all dance underground,
In their own party, silly sounds.

Mushrooms sport their polka dots,
While squirrels juggle shiny pots.
With every bud, a new joke's shared,
Nature's humor, it's never scared.

And as we witness life unfold,
Remember, laughter's worth its gold.
For in this dance of bright delight,
Each little giggle gives us flight!

Awakening Petals

The flowers yawn with morning light,
Stretching petals, what a sight!
Bees buzz by with playful glee,
"Hey there, dude! Come sip with me!"

Daisy sports a polka dot,
While Tulip claims, "I take the lot!"
Laughter swirls with the breeze,
As Pansy trips on clumsy knees.

The garden's now a lively stage,
Where every bloom is set to engage.
A comedy show of greens and hues,
With each new sprout, the fun ensues!

In the soil, the jokes take root,
Even dandelions can't stay mute!
They join the party, wild and bright,
"Who needs a lawn? We're out tonight!"

A Fresh Dawn Unfurled

Sunrise paints the world anew,
As clowns of color chase the dew.
Petals giggle, leaves crack jokes,
"Want a sip of morning's yokes?"

Worms wiggle in a wormy dance,
Frogs jump in as if by chance.
The birdies chatter up a storm,
Tweet-tweet-tweet, it's quite the norm!

Tulip's wearing a fancy hat,
While Sunflower flirts with the cat.
"Hey there, kitty, how's your day?"
"Paws off my spot, and go away!"

With giggles weaving through the air,
Nature's humor, everywhere!
So here's to laughter, bright and loud,
In our garden, we're all proud!

From Stillness to Splendor

In the quiet, whispers start,
Nudging seeds with tender heart.
A little sprout peeks from the ground,
"Did I just hear a silly sound?"

The ferns chuckle, sway and twist,
"Did you see that bumbling mist?"
As petals hum their merry tune,
A butterfly flirts with a balloon.

Ants parade in shiny rows,
"Excuse us, but we've got places to go!"
While ladybugs don their best bling,
Office workers of the spring!

The air buzzes with laughter bright,
As nature dances into the light.
From sleepy buds to splendor high,
Join the fun beneath the sky!

New Roots in Gentle Earth

Beneath the soil, a party brews,
New roots giggle in their shoes.
"Let's dig deep, it's kind of cool!"
"Watch my upward leap, it's a rule!"

Tiny critters join the fun,
"Who can find the biggest bun?"
The mushrooms dance and take a spin,
"Join us, friends, let's all begin!"

Sunbeams tickle all around,
Little hearts break from the ground.
"What's that sound? A sapling's cheer!"
"No more waiting, spring is here!"

Laughter echoes through the clumps,
As everyone joins in with jumps.
From tiny seeds to mighty gleams,
Here's to life and silly dreams!

The Promise of the Horizon

The sun peeks out like a shy little kid,
Asda wind tickles trees, and behold, they slid.
Persistence of nature, don't wear a frown,
The flowers erupt, like, 'Look at me now!'

Pollen parties start, all buzzing around,
Bees with tiny tuxedos, buzzing profound.
They drink up the nectar, dance with delight,
As the daisies giggle, 'We're ready for night!'

The First Gentle Stir

The ground does a wiggle, a joke on the grass,
As sproutlings pop out, saying, 'We'll pass!'
Worms wearing sunglasses crawl in the dirt,
Giving the flowers a muddy-alert.

The sun wakes up yawning, stretching so wide,
It spills golden giggles, brightening the tide.
A squirrel with acorns dons stylish flair,
While daisies roll over, 'Did he just stare?'

Incandescent Awakenings

In the garden, the laughter takes flight on a breeze,
Ladybugs with polka dots, strutting with ease.
Robins drop notes from their perch in the pine,
'Hey sun, have a dance, it's party time!'

Tulips wear tutus, swaying like pros,
While thistles are jiving beneath their fine bows.
'Oh snap!' says a cactus, 'I'm sharp, can't you see?'
But out here, we're friendly, just let it be me!'

Awakening Dreams

As shadows retreat, like a pajama parade,
The landscapes start giggling, no need to evade.
A butterfly flutters, donning a bow,
Saying, 'Watch this move, I'm stealing the show!'

The breeze plays the flute, the clouds clap along,
While the grass hums a tune, like it knows it belongs.
With every new petal, a whimsy unfurls,
As nature chuckles, 'Just watch how it twirls!'

Evocation of New Beginnings

The garden sprung with socks on trees,
A chorus of ants, one funny sneeze.
Cabbage in hats doing a jig,
While carrots roll out, they're feeling big.

Mice wear shades, they sashay about,
In a world where seeds wanna shout.
Turtles on skateboards zoom and roam,
Who knew the soil could feel like home?

Weeds don capes, they think they fly,
While the daisies dance, oh me, oh my!
The sun plays piano, what a sight,
As laughter prickles the morning light.

So here we toast to sprouts so wise,
In pots of joy, under sunny skies.
Every seedling grins, what a hoot!
In this crazy, green-rooted pursuit!

A Symphony of Awakening

Sapsuckers clapping with webbed feet,
Frogs join in with a ribbiting beat.
Daffodils prance, they're quite a show,
While butterflies wiggle with giddy glow.

Bunnies in bow ties hop and sway,
Planting their dreams in a lighthearted way.
The dawn wakes up with a giggle and pout,
While clouds play tag, no room for doubt.

Lemons wear smiles, their zesty delight,
As tomatoes burst forth, oh what a sight!
The whole garden chuckles, can't help but cheer,
For each tiny sprout that brings such good cheer.

So raise a glass to our garden pals,
With roots and rhymes, and green leafy gals.
May the laughter echo through sun and rain,
In our funny farm, where joy won't wane!

Where the Light Touches

Sunbeams tickle the tips of leaves,
While laughter echoes, each plant believes.
Twirling in shadows, the peas do a dance,
While celery jokes give the onions a chance.

The daisies paint smiles on the sky's cheek,
As radishes giggle, all joyful and sleek.
The breeze tells secrets to carrots anew,
While the broccoli poses, all proud in the view.

Fireflies tease, flickering at night,
While each little sprout feels perfectly bright.
In this wacky patch, the sun waves a hand,
Creating a stage where the flowers all stand.

Each petal holds stories, each leaf wears a grin,
In this green world of giggles, let's begin!
May the light keep shining, giving life a whirl,
Where every tiny sprout gives a twirl!

The Tender Touch of Life

Roses prance with a comic grace,
As daisies giggle, they keep up the race.
Every sprout's a jester in soil's ballet,
With each new bud, they laugh and play.

Sprinklers whistle a watery tune,
As worms hum along by the light of the moon.
Little buds wink, shake off their sleep,
While butterflies flit, their laughter runs deep.

Tomatoes declare with a fruity cheer,
In this patch of sunshine, there's nothing to fear.
The garden's a circus, a zany delight,
As the seeds all break out into wild flight.

To life's every question, let's give a cheer,
For the funny seasons, a bountiful year.
With joyous hearts and giggles in tow,
We celebrate sprouting, in sunlight's glow.

Sunlit Horizons

A sprout appears with a wink,
It thinks it's cooler than a drink.
With sunshine bathing its green cap,
It shouts, "Look out! I'm making a map!"

The daisies giggle, the roses tease,
"Hey, little sprout, catch a breeze!"
They dance around in joyful glee,
While the sprout just spills its tea.

Worms take bets on how tall it'll grow,
"Will it reach the clouds? Just wait and see!"
But with a wobble, it sways and bends,
And lands on a patch of its leafy friends.

The sun bids farewell, the moon peeks in,
"Let's keep growing; let the fun begin!"
Amidst the laughter, they start to cheer,
For all newcomers, there's nothing to fear.

Journey of the First Leaf

Once a bud, now is the case,
A leaf with quite the silly face.
It dances on the morning breeze,
And tickles ants beneath the trees.

With a flip and a flop, it takes a ride,
On a squirrel's back, the leaf won't hide.
"Let's go explore!" it dares to shout,
Thinks it's the king of all that's about!

They tumble and roll through the grass so bright,
While other leaves watch with pure delight.
"What a team! Who needs a plan?"
They giggle and spin, the world's their land.

As twilight comes, they grab their hats,
Sharing stories with chirpy little chats.
A leaf and a squirrel, what a pair,
Heartily laughing without a care.

Rebirth in Ribbons

Wrapped in colors, the flowers cheer,
"What's that sound? Oh, it's springtime near!"
With ribbons glimmering in the sun,
They twirl around, oh what fun!

The tulips hum a jazzy tune,
While daisies boogie beneath the moon.
"Who needs silence?" they sing with glee,
As butterflies join in the jamboree.

The daisies wear hats, all frilly and bright,
And make-believe they're stars of the night.
With petals flapping to the beat,
They dance on air, oh what a feat!

In this vibrant garden, joy's found a seat,
With laughter and prancing, life's a treat.
Wrapped in ribbons, they'll spin and sway,
For fun's the language of flowers today!

The Prelude of Petals

A petal fell with a funny plop,
It rolled around, then did a hop.
"Hey, everyone, come see my trick!"
The other flowers giggled and picked.

In a garden where daisies dress with flair,
The colorful show began to declare.
"Petal, oh Petal, how do you play?"
"I'm just warming up, don't throw me away!"

They gathered 'round for a flower spree,
With pollen as confetti, they danced with glee.
A trumpet vine plays a jazzy tune,
While the petals rent the warm afternoon.

As laughter blooms, they form a pact,
"We'll flaunt our colors—no turning back!"
In a prelude for petals, they make a stand,
For fun's the magic in this vibrant land.

Roots that Reach

Deep in the ground, they wiggle with glee,
Searching for snacks—oh, what a spree!
They tickle the soil, they play hide and seek,
Hoping for sunlight, just a little peek.

Worms throw them parties, a root celebration,
With laughter and joy—what a sensation!
Each sprout wears a hat made of dirt,
Joking with flowers, "You can't be worse!"

Tiny little roots stretch out every day,
"Don't mind us, we're just here to play!"
They tickle the toes of passing ants,
While dancing to music—oh, what a chance!

In a garden where everything grows,
They poke out their heads, strike silly poses.
With each twist and turn, they welcome the light,
Saying, "We're roots, and we're feeling quite bright!"

The Dance of the Unseen

In shadows they jiggle, the seeds below,
Twisting and turning in a secret show.
They dream of the sun but keep it hush-hush,
Practicing moves in the midnight rush.

With a wiggle and giggle, they start to rehearse,
A dance for the flowers, oh isn't it terse?
They poke through the dirt in a playful race,
"Look at us twirling, it's quite the chase!"

Invisible partners join in the fun,
Caterpillars slide as they welcome the sun.
"Let's throw a soirée," giggled the chill,
With roots and elves, oh what a thrill!

When morning arrives, the blossoms take flight,
Joined by the dancers who leaped in the night.
With shades of green swaying and twisting with flair,
"Who knew all the magic was hidden down there?"

A Canvas of Colors

Splash a little yellow, a sprinkle of blue,
A dazzle of orange, and maybe a hue!
The flowers all giggle, "Oh what a sight,
We're the artists of sunshine, painting delight!"

With petals like brushes, they dance in the breeze,
"Paint us in purple, or with stripes, if you please!"
A sunflower whispers, "I'll go for a crown,
And steal the bright spotlight from the whole town!"

The daisies all chuckle, "Who said we're plain?
We'll throw in some polka dots with no shame!"
Together they sparkle, a rainbow divine,
Swaying and singing, "We're flavors of time!"

In this vibrant garden, laughter's the thread,
Creating a tapestry where dreams are fed.
And as day ends, their colors won't fade,
For the joy that they gift is forever displayed!

Radiance in Rebirth

With each new spring, there's a tickle in air,
A party for plants; it's beyond compare!
They stretch out their limbs, all covered in dew,
Looking around, saying, "What's fresh and new?"

A cactus joins in, "I'm sharp but not shy!
I'll show you my blooms—a bright fashion high!"
While tulips all giggle with petals like skirts,
Dancing in rhythm, no need for alerts!

"Let's host a reunion!" the daisies declare,
Filling the garden with tales to share.
"We've been hiding away, but look at us now,
With boldness and laughter, we take a bow!"

In this show of rebirth, they laugh very loud,
Welcoming bees in a colorful crowd.
With sunshine to guide them, their spirits will thrive,
"Oh, what a riot!" they sing, feeling alive!

Petals of Promise

In a garden where socks disappear,
Daisies dance with joy and cheer.
Bees in bow ties buzz with flair,
Pretending to be debonair.

A sunflower wears a hat so wide,
While tulips gossip, side by side.
Each petal beams, a smile so bright,
Who knew plants could be such a sight?

They plan a party, a wild affair,
With fruit punch served in a watering can there.
Chickens in tuxedos, a sight so absurd,
Join the laughter, oh how they stir!

So come and witness this silly spree,
Where every plant is as wacky as can be.
In nature's club, nobody's shy,
So grab a bloom and give it a try!

Fresh Starts in Starlight

In a world where snails race cars,
The moon shines down on chocolate bars.
Starry-eyed petals sway with glee,
Planning to dance under the cherry tree.

With fireflies dressed as twinkling sprites,
They kick off a bash, oh what delights!
A rhubarb pie spun from laughter bright,
Fills the air with pure delight.

Each leaf assumes a funky stance,
As crickets creep in, they start to prance.
Laughter echoes, a joyous choir,
In this garden, they never tire.

So if you hear a rustling beat,
Know the flowers are tapping their feet.
Under starlit skies, they burst and sing,
In their world, every day is spring!

The Garden of Hope

In a quirky plot of crafty woes,
Grew a carrot dressed like a rose.
The radishes rolled their eyes with fun,
While lettuce rapped 'bout the morning sun.

A worm in shades offers words of wisdom,
"Life's a ride, just find your rhythm!"
With petals giggling at the silly sight,
They host a gala each starry night.

Frogs in tuxedos leap with zest,
Chasing down the snails in their quest.
Every bloom whispers a funny tale,
Of mischief and laughter that never fails.

So plant your seeds of humor deep,
And let your garden giggle and leap.
For in this patch, joy takes its throne,
With laughter, it's never alone!

Fragile Tendrils

Tiny tendrils twist and sway,
Unruly weeds just want to play.
In sneakers, roots grant them a race,
While butterflies giggle, keeping pace.

With a crackle of laughter and a flip of a leaf,
They stretch up high, beyond belief.
The sun winks back with a golden grin,
As flowers bloom, let the fun begin!

In pots, their dreams take off like kites,
Sharing secrets under starlit nights.
With dirt on their cheeks, they're cute and spry,
Planting giggles as they reach for the sky.

Join this frolic, don't miss the chance,
To grow some joy and join the dance.
For every tendril that stretches wide,
Holds a story that cannot hide!

Fluttering into Existence

Tiny buds stretch, I must admit,
Cracking open, they throw a fit.
In the garden where laughter rings,
Plants gossip about the silliest things.

Ladybugs dance, wiggling in style,
While caterpillars munch in a silly guile.
A bird chirps a joke, oh what a tease,
Nature's comedy, a breeze with ease.

Colors pop out, a paint splash spree,
Dandelions giggle right next to the bee.
Who knew blooms had a sense of fun?
Sunshine and laughter, their favorite run.

With each petal and leaf, the joy unfurls,
A world full of laughter, it twirls and whirls.
Watch the sprouts wiggle and shake in delight,
In a wacky parade, all day and all night.

Crafting New Chapters

Once upon a seed, a tale begins,
Sprouted dreams with cheery grins.
Plot twists in soil, roots intertwined,
Every leaf a page, truly defined.

A squirrel in the shade, he reads with glee,
Critters gather 'round for a fun story spree.
Branches becoming characters, quirky and bold,
In the book of life, new words unfold.

Rain drops like ink on the chapter's edge,
While sunbeams offer a bright pledge.
Each bloom a punchline, a twist in the jest,
A merry adventure, never a rest.

So gather your laughter, let stories out,
In this quirky tale, there's no room for doubt.
With every new bud, a chuckle we find,
Crafting new chapters, oh so kind.

The Lullaby of Growth

Whispers of green in the soft morning light,
Nature sings gently, it's quite a delight.
Dewdrops are tickling the petals so small,
While worms share secrets and giggle with all.

In the arms of the breeze, young shoots sway and sway,
Frogs croaking tunes in their own ribbit way.
A symphony formed by the buzzing of bees,
Crickets keep time—imagine the tease!

The chorus of sprouts hums a tune,
Dancing with daisies beneath the full moon.
Every root takes a step in this whimsical dance,
Moments of laughter give fortune a chance.

In the garden of giggles, all troubles are small,
Growing together, we'll stand ever tall.
So sing with the flowers, let your spirit flow,
In our lullaby of growth, let joy overflow.

A Whiff of Newness

A sweet little whiff of something fresh,
A quirk in the air, with an aromatic mesh.
Breezes are teasing, turning heads in delight,
As new buds wiggle, they're ready for flight.

Petals are playful, donning their best,
Tickling the senses—what an odd fest!
The grass tells jokes while the flowers chime in,
A comedy club, beneath the great kin.

With every new sprout, an aroma so bright,
It fills up the air, quite a wonderful sight.
Silly scents swirl, perhaps lavender dreams,
Every corner bursting with fragrant themes.

In this cheerful place, where humor unmasks,
Newness is fun, freeing us from tasks.
So take a deep breath, let the laughter ensue,
A whiff of newness, how refreshing and true!

The Gentle Thaw

The snowmen droop like sad old clowns,
Their carrot noses footballs falling down.
The sun breaks through with a goofy grin,
And melts away all the winter's sin.

Puddles splash like laughter on the ground,
While everyone jumps with joy unbound.
Silly hats abandoned in the sun,
It's time for warmth and a little fun!

Flip-flops dance as the jackets retreat,
Ice cream cones instead of frozen feet.
Nature chuckles, shedding winter's coat,
As springs pull up in a lively boat.

So bring your socks and your rainbow ties,
Let's celebrate with bright, funny skies!
The thawing brings giggles, oh what a riot,
Springtime's here—let's start a quiet diet!

In the Shade of Fresh Starts

A tree awakens with a stretch and yawn,
Dancing leaves, like they've just been drawn.
Squirrels plot with mischievous intent,
In the warmth of sun, their energy's spent.

The flowers giggle, colors come alive,
Petals and pollen start to connive.
Bees are buzzing, they've a busy plan,
With tiny top hats, they make quite a span.

In this garden of chuckles, bees do break,
Carrying tunes only they can make.
Each little sprout has a story to share,
Of bumbles and tumbles without a care.

Dandelions pop like jokes in the breeze,
While butterflies float with relative ease.
Let's toast with lemonade to sunny rays,
In the shade of a tree, let silliness stay!

The Color of Hope

A painter strolls with a cheeky smirk,
Splashing colors where shadows lurk.
The dullest gray has thrown in the towel,
Pink polka dots making quite the growl.

The sun is a brush, swirling cheer on high,
While rainbows giggle, spreading laughter nigh.
Frogs in bow ties jump in puddles of blue,
Making ripples of joy, oh what a view!

With every stroke, a prank is revealed,
Nature's canvas, hilarity sealed.
Clouds wear their hats made of cotton and fluff,
Painting the sky—a bit silly, but tough.

So here's to the hues that bring us delight,
A palette of chuckles, from morning to night.
Let's splash through life with a vibrant spree,
For in every color, there's fun, can't you see?

Renewal's Serenade

The morning wakes, with a stretch and a sneeze,
While birds strike a pose, as cool as you please.
Their songs sound like giggles, a musical tease,
As blooms join in chorus, swaying with ease.

In forests, the critters have fancy affairs,
Throwing tiny gatherings, full of wild dares.
Rabbits wear slippers, and owls don their ties,
While squirrels share gossip, with winks and sly sighs.

The breeze joins the party, fluttering near,
Whispering secrets that only we hear.
With a wink and a nod, the world comes alive,
In wooly thoughts, we are bound to thrive.

So let's dance beneath this joyous parade,
With a jig and a smile, no masquerade.
Nature's own serenade—can't resist,
In this silly renewal, let's all coexist!

The Dawn's Tender Embrace

The sun peeks out from under the sheets,
Yawning loudly, it stumbles on its feet.
Birds chirp loudly, they've had their coffee,
Singing tunes that are slightly off-key.

The flowers stretch and give a little sway,
While the grass giggles, inviting play.
A butterfly trips in a curious twirl,
Dressing up in colors, it starts to swirl.

The clouds float by, puffy and white,
Playing peek-a-boo, oh what a sight!
A squirrel drops acorns, creates a mess,
Then strikes a pose like a funny guest.

With laughter echoing in the fresh air,
Nature's comedy show is laying bare.
So let's roll with joy like kids on the slides,
In this grand performance where fun collides.

New Horizons in Green

New leaves sprout like hair from a dome,
Each one whispering, 'Let's leave our home!'
Amidst the chaos, the worms dance and spin,
Rehearsing their moves with a cheeky grin.

Ants march onwards, like soldiers on parade,
Carrying snacks, they're never dismayed.
A dandelion giggles, puffing out seeds,
Telling the winds, 'Take care of my needs!'

Chirping crickets audition for fame,
With legs that scratch, they'd win any game.
A small frog jumps, its landing a flop,
But it's still the star of the hop-along bop!

As laughter springs forth from every green vine,
Even the rocks feel a little divine.
In this patch of green, hilarity reigns,
Where every critter has laughter in chains.

Kaleidoscope of the Unsung

In the meadow where colors collide,
Grasshoppers giggle, they can't run and hide.
A flower shouts, 'Pick me, I'm the best!'
While a snail slowly wins in the slowest test.

Bees buzz about with nectar-filled dreams,
Racing, yet tangled in sticky routines.
A ladybug chuckles, snapping a joke,
Encouraging laughter, around it, folks poke.

The wind carries whispers of things out of sight,
Birds gossip loudly, they're soaring in flight.
A butterfly stumbles, loses its grace,
Then strikes a pose, quite the silly face!

As dusk starts to settle, the stars play their part,
Joking with each other, they're artful and smart.
In this sketch of nature, a laugh we can share,
A kaleidoscope spinning with joy in the air.

Sprouts of Hope

Tiny seeds burrow, whisper their dreams,
Sprouting through soil, they burst at the seams.
A sunflower grins, it's tall and quite proud,
While nearby, a weed throws a wild crowd.

A carrot giggles, underground it sleeps,
Waiting for someone, to pull from the deeps.
That eager rabbit hops in to munch,
But the carrot winks—'I'm not for lunch!'

With each little sprout, there's a story to tell,
Some silly, some serious, all doing quite well.
The rain falls down like nature's sweet tears,
Dancing in puddles, quelling our fears.

And as they all grow into something so fine,
The garden is laughing, just sipping on wine.
With roots all entwined, they share the rapport,
Sprouts of delight, leaving us wanting more!

Nature's New Narrative

Tiny buds dance in the breeze,
Squirrels plotting mischief with ease.
Butterflies try to find their wing,
While flowers giggle, and robins sing.

Dandelions wear their seeds like hats,
While ants organize their garden chats.
Grasshoppers leap in a silly parade,
Nature's tale is a circus well-made.

Bees buzzing with a sweet tooth knack,
Chasing nectar, they never look back.
A worm winks from beneath the earth,
Claiming his title, king of rebirth.

Dusting Off the Dreams

Yesterday's thoughts are in a pile,
Grass stains on pants with a cheeky smile.
Waking up from hibernation,
With plans for reckless creation.

Socks mismatched and full of cheer,
Spring's wild spirit is finally here.
Kites in the air, pulling on strings,
While laughter floats, and freedom sings.

Dust off the daisies and let's take flight,
Turning mundane moments into delight.
Worms with sunglasses, what a sight!
Dreams are dusty, but still feel right.

A Tapestry of New Growth

Caterpillars painting their masterpieces,
While puppies sprout up like mini ceases.
The rainbow plays peek-a-boo with the sun,
And daisies whisper, 'This is just fun!'

Silly ants in their disco groove,
Flipping leaves in a wild, dance move.
Weeds audition for a role in the show,
While garden gnomes take it nice and slow.

Bumblebees juggle while sipping their tea,
What a ruckus in the green jubilee!
Blossoms gossip in ruffled attire,
Tickling the breeze with every desire.

Awash with Potential

Puddles giggle as splashes unfold,
Best friends with clouds, so brave and bold.
Seeds get raucous, they're set to ignite,
Sowing wild dreams under starlit night.

Chickens launching their morning debate,
"Who's got the loudest cluck, can't wait!"
Sprouts poke through like curious heads,
Wondering if life's better out of their beds.

Trees sharing secrets in rustling cheer,
The humor of nature is so crystal clear.
Like socks left unmatched, or popsicles that melt,
Every tiny moment's a treasure we felt.

www.ingramcontent.com/pod-product-compliance
Lightning Source LLC
Chambersburg PA
CBHW072123070526
44585CB00016B/1543